Remmy: A Hero Dog of War

Remmy: A Hero Dog of War

PRISCILLA MILLER

ISBN: 1535367776
ISBN 13: 9781535367776

Doug Davis is the owner of DeWitt Marine, situated on the Clam River in northern Michigan. On most days his Dutch Shepherd Remmy, a retired patrol explosive detection dog (PEDD), accompanied him to the marina, and while Doug worked at his desk, the dog would lie on the floor next to his chair.

Doug Davis in his office, with Remmy at his side.

Photos of other military service dogs hang on Doug's office wall.

The office walls are lined with photos of other military service dogs, and one photo in particular shows Doug when he was younger, dressed in a military uniform with a magnificent German Shepherd at his side. Doug, a former air force dog handler, enlisted in the air force in 1966, never thinking at the time that he would end up serving more than three hundred nights in the bush outside the wire, doing perimeter security at Phu Cat, in the Binh Dinh Province of Vietnam.

Upon graduation from basic training, he served several months working at the main gate and riding patrol at Seymour Johnson Air Force Base. That's when he finally decided that law enforcement wasn't for him and switched to working security. It only took him one night of walking around a squadron of F-100s for him to say to himself, "I'm out of here," and he volunteered for canine. His squadron commander tried to talk him out of canine by telling him he would be shipped to Vietnam, but by that time, Doug knew it really didn't matter. He had already figured out that everyone on the base would be going to Vietnam, and he had made up his mind that he would rather have a dog next to him than be in a bunker by himself.

He attended "dog school" at Lackland Air Force Base, in San Antonio, Texas, where dogs from all five branches of the military were trained. Since each dog had a different way of alerting during training, it could take several months of working with a dog for its handler to become familiar with his dog's alerting behavior. The dogs sent to Vietnam were trained to perform specific jobs. Sentry dogs defended the perimeter of military bases and were their first line of defense, as they "walked the wire" on the perimeter of the bases, ammo depots, and other sensitive areas. Their mission was to detect, detain, and destroy. Tracker dogs were used to track the enemy and locate downed pilots and missing or wounded personnel by using either airborne or ground scents. Scout dogs were sent out with an infantry company on patrols and served as their eyes and ears, as they "walked point" (out front) of the unit. According to Doug, they always tried to work downwind, and once a dog alerted, the handler, after determining the direction of the dog's alert, used hand signals to alert the unit, who, if needed, brought in tracker dogs to locate the enemy. They also alerted their handlers to ambushes and booby traps and were used to pursue fleeing ambushers and to locate lost soldiers and downed aircraft.

While Doug was stationed at Phu Cat, which was located seventeen miles northwest of Quin Nhon, he and his sentry dog, Smoke, joined a team of thirty-eight dog handlers and their dogs. Their assignment was to secure the perimeter of the base at night. The "dog men," as they were called, patrolled outside the twenty-seven miles of concertina wire that encircled the base and actually ventured some distance into the surrounding jungle in search of Viet Cong. Once they were locked and loaded, on their way outside of the wire, the men in the bunkers would say, "Hey, dog men, stay on your toes tonight." They knew if the enemy breached their security, all hell would break loose!

When alerting on an animal, Smoke made a weaving motion, but when alerting on a human, he would walk straight forward. One day while on patrol, Smoke exhibited a strange, dance-like alert, leaving Doug totally confused by his dog's bizarre behavior. It was then that he noticed the dog was standing on an anthill and being attacked by an army of fire ants. He quickly jerked on Smoke's six-foot leash, pulling him away from the anthill, and that was when something totally unexpected happened. The metal clasp on the leash snapped apart, leaving Doug to quickly fashion a makeshift leash and then head back to base for a new one.

Several days later, while a captured Viet Cong officer was being interrogated, he recounted an incident that had happened a few days prior to his capture. It seemed his men were about to fire on a dog handler when the handler experienced an "equipment failure" (Smoke's leash breaking); rather than prematurely expose their position, he ordered his men to stand down, allowing the handler to return to base. That was almost forty years ago, but Doug has never forgotten that fateful day, and he knows if that leash had not broken, he wouldn't be here today.

Doug in Vietnam with his sentry dog Smoke.

During wartime, dogs were the most effective device for saving lives. They braved countless dangers to bring our men home alive. Their sense of smell is said to be one thousand times greater than humans, and they can sniff out the enemy up to one thousand yards away. Dogs are credited with reducing casualties by 65 percent in the areas of Vietnam where they served. The dogs were hated by the Viet Cong so much that they offered rewards for a handler's uniform patch or the tattooed ear from a dog. Reports of dogs saving the lives of their handlers were common. In one such incident, the dog alerted, but the handler, not seeing anything, was about to step forward when the dog blocked his path. It was then that the handler noticed a trip wire hidden in the jungle foliage. Another example of the devotion shared between these dogs of war and their handlers occurred when a handler lay critically injured and felt his life ebbing away. He ordered his dog to leave, but the dog refused to obey and instead grasped his handler's collar in his teeth and began dragging him out of harm's way. The dog, despite being wounded himself, continued on until they reached safety. When the handler's condition had been stabilized at a field hospital, he insisted on seeing his dog before being shipped to a military hospital for further treatment. After a brief reunion, the two parted and were never to see each other again, leaving the handler to always wonder whatever happened to his brave companion.

Dogs were considered disposable "military equipment." Doug was relieved to learn that Smoke had become ill while in Vietnam and had been euthanized, because the dogs remaining after the war were turned over to the Vietnamese, where in all likelihood they ended up as someone's dinner.

*According to US War Dogs Association Inc., it is estimated that approximately 4,900 dogs where used during the course of the war between

1964 and 1975. Only 204 dogs exited Vietnam during the ten-year pe-
riod. Some remained in the Pacific, and some returned to the United
States. None returned to civilian life. So what happened to the dogs
that remained? Most were euthanized, and the others were turned over
to the ARVN (South Vietnamese Army). It is estimated that these dogs
saved more than ten thousand lives.

*The "Not Forgotten Fountain" is part of the US Military Working Dog Teams'
National monument in San Antonio. Photo by Paula Slater*

Doug with Ringo, his adopted navy dog

RINGO

In 1970 Doug was discharged from the air force and returned home to his wife and civilian life. He raised a family and built a business, but throughout those years, the memories of his time in Vietnam with Smoke always remained fresh in his mind, and he would not allow himself to grow attached to another dog. Then in 2008 he received a call from Louisa Kastner, of Mission K-9 Rescue (formerly Military Working Dogs Adoptions). She told him that it was time for him to adopt a retired military working dog, and she eventually convinced him to do just that. In November, a navy dog named Ringo, who had served in Kuwait, came to live with Doug and Pam. Pam said, "He was an escape artist, and his mischievous behavior stole our hearts." Sadly in 2011, Ringo became ill and had to be put down. The Davises were so devastated by his loss that Pam told Doug, "Never again," and he agreed.

There was something about one dog with its head cocked to the side.

Never Say "Never!"

In July of 2012, Doug once again received several e-mails from Louisa. They contained photos of several retired military service dogs that needed homes. One of the photos in particular caught his eye. There was just something about one dog lying in the back of a truck with his head cocked to the side that made him stop and realize that he and Pam still had "a hell lot more to give." After talking it over, they decided to give it another shot, and they opened their hearts and home to Remmy. When a retired military working dog is adopted, little, if anything, is ever known about its past history or the identity of its handler. Doug was fortunate to receive a couple of photos taken of Remmy with an unidentified handler in Afghanistan. He was also told that Remmy was responsible for preventing multiple casualties when he alerted on a village hut rigged with explosives set to go off when the door they were about to enter was opened.

Doug also received a photo of Remmy with his handlers in Afghanistan.

LIFE WITH REMMY

No one seemed to know how long Remmy had been confined in a kennel, but it was obvious he had received little, if any, human interaction. All the months he must have spent in captivity took a toll, because by the time this once-active dog finally came to live with the Davises, all of his teeth were worn down to nothing. Frustration and boredom had left him with nothing to do but gnaw on his stainless steel food bowl and the chain-link fence that held him captive. Shortly after his arrival, he had to undergo oral surgery and have the remnants of his teeth removed.

Remmy sleeping off the aftereffects of oral surgery.

At first Doug was a bit concerned about leaving Pam at home alone with Remmy while he was away at work, but it wasn't long before it became apparent that Remmy and Pam had become the best of friends. Making friends with Doc, the family cat, however, was another matter. Doc was used to being around Ringo and, as a result, had no fear of the new dog. Remmy, on the other hand, did not care for Doc at all. If Remmy still had had his teeth, Doc might not have fared so well, but when Doc walked over to greet him, Remmy only ended up with a mouthful of Doc's fur. For about six weeks after that, Remmy was kept on a leash, until he finally realized that Doc was also a member of the Davis family and must be tolerated. A truce eventually developed between the two of them, and Remmy learned to ignore Doc, even when the vocal feline would go up to him while he was sleeping and meow in his ear.

A truce eventually occurred between Remmy and Doc.

In spite of being toothless, Remmy still enjoyed spending endless hours gnawing on his favorite Kong, but above all else, he loved going for rides. As soon as anyone opened the front door, Remmy was on his way out the door, ready to jump in the family van. Soon he was riding with Doug to work or accompanying Pam on her daily errands.

Life with Remmy proved to be an adventure and often reminded Pam of the days when her triplets were toddlers. He didn't like being alone and had to know where she was at all times. As a result he followed her everywhere she went, even to the bathroom, where he would sit outside the door patiently waiting for her. He loved going for rides in the car with her, and if she didn't take him with her, she would arrive home to find him sulking. He always accompanied the Davises when they visited their chiropractor, and while there, he even received his own special massage.

Remmy loved wearing his service-dog vest. (He was a registered mobility dog, used for stabilizing people with balance difficulties.) As soon as it was put on him, he instinctively knew he was working and was able to accompany Pam into public buildings where dogs were not normally allowed.

Pam knew it would always take longer when shopping with Remmy, because people always wanted to stop and talk to her or ask to pet him. So on days when she wasn't in a hurry, she would take him with her. He had a habit of sniffing the feet of everyone who walked by, and she was concerned about what in the world she would ever do if he were to sit and alert on one of the store's customers. She finally decided if that ever did happen, she would contact the manager and let him or her know that her dog had detected someone who might have explosives on them.

Bank tellers at the local bank adored Remmy and they always had treats for him. He looked forward to going behind the counter to greet them. One day, surprised customers pulled up to the drive-through window on a day Remmy was visiting and were greeted by him standing up on his hind legs, looking out the teller's window at them.

Remmy loved wearing his service vest.

Remmy soon became best friends with their neighbor's dog Max and would often go over to visit him. Max's owner had a lovely garden that reflected her expertise as a master gardener. Remmy and Max would run around, having a great time, and ultimately end up trampling through the garden as the neighbor yelled at them to get out. Remmy also liked to sneak over to her garden every chance he got and fertilize it. Doug would quickly grab his shovel and try to remove the evidence before the neighbor discovered it.

One day, Pam and Doug became very concerned when they couldn't find Remmy and he didn't come when called. They began searching for him, fearing he might have run down to the main road. Just as they were about to jump into their van and drive down to the road, their neighbor noticed the screen door on his home was ajar. When he went inside the house, there was Remmy, stretched out on the floor, making himself right at home.

Remmy loved delivery people, because everyone—including the UPS, FedEx drivers, the mail carrier, and even the trash pickup man—always had treats for him. On one occasion, he startled the FedEx delivery driver when he jumped into the truck, sat down, and alerted on a package. Pam had to explain to the driver that Remmy was a bomb-detection dog. Closer examination of the package showed that it contained a shipment of ammunition coming from Cabela's.

When a handyman came to retile the bath, he brought his tools into the house without incident, but when he attempted to carry a drop cloth into the house, Remmy barked and wouldn't let him pass. Pam was certain that the drop cloth must have reminded him of a burka. Once the drop cloth was neatly folded, he allowed the worker into the house without further incident.

One day while Doug was visiting his next-door neighbor, Remmy ran into the neighbor's garage and alerted on something.

He refused to budge, even when Doug called him. When he finally did come out of the garage, he had something in his mouth, and it was then that Doug discovered he had one of his neighbor's tennis balls. From then on, tennis balls proved to be Remmy's favorite toy, and Doug always made sure he had an abundant supply of them on hand.

Tennis balls were his favorite toy.

News always has a way of traveling fast in a small town, and word of Doug Davis adopting another retired military working dog soon spread. When the writer for a local newspaper heard the news, she was curious and thought there might be a story waiting for her to tell. After talking with Doug and meeting Remmy, she was amazed to learn of the contributions these brave K-9s have made during times of war and realized how many other people like herself must be totally unaware of the thousands of lives military working dogs were responsible for saving. She decided to tell their story. Doug let her borrow the photos taken of Remmy with his handler in Afghanistan, and they were used in the article.

In 2012 "Hero Dogs of War" was featured on the front page of the August 30 issue of the *Elk Rapids News*. The article was also posted on the Internet.

SERENDIPITY

(The dictionary defines "serendipity" as the occurrence and development of events by chance in a happy or beneficial way.)

Over a year had passed since the feature story on Remmy first appeared in the newspaper, and things in the Davis household had settled into a normal everyday routine. Doug and Pam knew their new family member was a war hero and often wondered where his handler was and wished Remmy could share his war stories with them. Imagine their surprise when one day in late October, Doug received an e-mail from a man identifying himself as Dan, Remmy's handler in Afghanistan. He explained that over six years had passed since he had returned to the United States, leaving Remmy behind in Afghanistan. During that time, he often wondered what happened to him, but repeated attempts at trying to locate his old partner over the Internet always proved futile, and he eventually figured Remmy was no longer alive and finally quit searching.

He went on to explain that while surfing the web that day, he inadvertently clicked on a link and to his amazement, there was the "Hero Dogs of War" story, containing the photo of himself with Remmy in Afghanistan. After a phone call or two, Dan had managed to track down Doug, and a short time later, he sent the e-mail. Later that evening they were on the phone. Doug listened intently as Dan told him about Remmy's heroics. Not only had Remmy prevented twelve men in a patrol unit from entering a hut rigged with explosives, but he also learned that the docile dog, now curled up and sleeping in front of the fireplace once had the reputation of being a warrior's warrior and that the men knew they could always rely on Remmy. When it came to detecting explosives, he was 100 percent accurate every time. Whenever he froze in his tracks and pointed his nose in a specific direction, an explosive device was always located in the area he alerted on. According to Dan, "Remmy never trusted Afghans, and he was credited with at least eleven combat bites" (which translates into the number of Taliban he brought down by himself). In fact, he was so notorious and hated by the Taliban that a wanted poster was circulated, offering a $10,000 reward for proof of the demise of Remmy and his handler. At the end of their phone conversation, the two men agreed to meet in person.

This docile dog curled up in front of the fireplace was once considered a warrior's warrior.

Reunion

Just prior to Thanksgiving, Doug and his K-9 companion drove from their home in northern Michigan to Grand Rapids for a meeting with Dan, who drove up from the Chicago area. Tears filled the eyes of those who watched as Dan, who thought he would never see Remmy again, entered the room. Seeing him for the first time in years, Dan called out to him, "Remmy Boy." Hearing that old familiar voice speak his name stirred something in the recesses of the dog's memory and he left Doug's side, went over to Dan, gave him a sniff of recognition, and then leaned up against him. Dan knelt down, put his arms around Remmy, and hugged him. Later that evening, the two men took Remmy outdoors. That's when the former Vietnam-era dog handler turned to Remmy's former handler and offered him the dog's leash. Dan eagerly took it in his hand and proceeded to walk into a nearby field with Remmy. Doug stayed back and stood watching as the two old partners walked side by side once again, and in that moment, he could see that the handler and his dog had stepped back in time for a few minutes and were a team once again.

Dan and Remmy together again!

Dan and Doug meet for the first time.

Remmy in Afghanistan

Before long many of the questions Doug and Pam had about Remmy were answered, as Dan began telling Doug his story. Originally he had trained with a dog named Bear, who was a good dog in training, but when they arrived in Afghanistan, he wouldn't pay attention to Dan and had to be washed out of the program. Dan was without a dog for several days, but then Remmy's handler was promoted to kennel master, and Remmy was left without a handler. Dan began working with Remmy, and they proved to be a perfect match. Remmy always tried to please Dan, who by then knew he had a perfect working military dog. They were the first working military dog team to take part in the concept of using IED (improvised explosive device) detection dog teams in Afghanistan.

When they arrived at Firebase Tycz, unit 88291 was there. The unit had just taken part in the battle of Tribeca Pass, and they had all been awarded Silver Stars. Dan, with a new dog, described feeling like a schmuck and was afraid he would mess up. On their first mission, less than a mile from the main gate, Remmy alerted, indicating there was an IED in the middle of the road. At first, Dan wasn't sure. He thought it was too close to the base and that maybe Remmy was mistaken, so he brought Remmy back and began the search again. Once again, Remmy alerted on the same area. Dan moved forward a couple of steps and maintained security while the engineer walked up. They both tried to look cool despite the fact that everyone in the convoy, many who were already skeptical about using dogs to sniff out IEDs, watched them. Both men got down on their knees and began digging with their bare hands. Then much to their relief, they touched metal. Remmy locating that bomb gained the novice team a whole lot of respect that day.

The next day, as they were checking out the compound that over-looked the IED site, they conducted a "soft knock," knocking on doors and asking the occupants if they had seen or heard anything pertaining to that IED. They separated the men and women in the compound and began to search it. As they were about to leave, someone noticed Remmy sitting in front of a trash can. When they checked it, they found aluminum foil wrappers used to construct the IED. Once again, Remmy had proved himself to be an exceptional IED detection dog.

On their next mission, they dismounted from their vehicles and walked to the center of a small town, which was located around a fountain and a well. As they approached the fountain, they became the target of small-arms fire. They immediately broke, took up positions as trained, and returned fire. Dan was running down an alley, and because he was a right-handed shooter, he automatically looked to his left, leaving his right side vulnerable to attack. An Afghani suddenly jumped out on Dan's blind side with a gun in his hand. Remmy immediately reacted, lunging at the Afghani and bringing him down to the ground—at which point Dan was then able to finish the engagement. He said, "It was just another example of Remmy understanding the task at hand and executing it flawlessly." They secured the town, and further investigation of the store they originally came to search revealed a treasure trove of bomb-making materials, manuals, propaganda, and also heroin. They also discovered "Wanted Dead or Alive" posters for the "bearded American and his dog." Dan had to admit that seeing himself and Remmy on the posters was not a very good feeling.

A welcome drink at the well on a very hot day.

The "bearded American and his dog" were wanted, dead or alive.

AMBUSH

September 17, 2004, began like any other day. Before every mission, Dan and Remmy had a routine of getting "jocked up." They would go back to their room and put on their gear and vests. Once Remmy was jocked up, his entire demeanor changed. The hackles on his back would stand straight up, and his muscles would engorge, making him appear much larger and meaner. He knew they were going out on a mission, and he was ready to go to work. Temperatures in that region of Afghanistan ranged from 100 to 120 degrees all summer long and well into October. After loading up about 150 pounds of their gear, they headed out with another dog-handler team joining them.

All "jocked up"

19

On this mission they headed out together with the dogs kenneled in the back of their Land Rover. Just as they reached the dip of a hill, they hit an IED, and Dan and the other handler were thrown up in the air and slammed to the ground. As they limped away from what was left of their vehicle, their thoughts immediately turned to the dogs, but miraculously the dogs had escaped injury.

Examination of the IED remnants determined that it had been an armed, pressure-detonated IED made from a 106 Russian artillery shell. Since multiple vehicles had rolled over the same spot, it was apparent that the K-9 vehicle had been the target.

Both men suffered serious injuries to their legs and feet, requiring them to be medevacked to a hospital in Germany. After several months, Dan returned to Afghanistan and to an exuberant welcome from Remmy. Their second deployment was even more successful, with Remmy being responsible for a total of eleven "combat bites" (the number of times he brought down the enemy). He also discovered multiple IEDs and was no longer eyed with suspicion or made the butt of jokes. IED dogs by this time had made a name for themselves and were highly respected.

The dogs were kenneled in the back of the Land Rover
when the K-9 Vehicle was targeted.

Time to Say Good-Bye

The day finally arrived when Dan had to transition out of the military and leave Remmy behind. They returned to Kandahar, where the new handler began training with Remmy and bonding with him. For several days, whenever Dan walked past Remmy's kennel, he would whine, and Dan would go over and visit him. The new handler finally had to inform Dan that he was now Remmy's handler and that Dan was not helping him adjust to the change. Dan described the day he finally said good-bye to Remmy as one of the roughest days in his life.

Saying good-bye was the hardest thing Dan ever had to do.

News Travels Fast!

When news of Remmy and Dan's reunion was posted on Facebook, a platoon sergeant with the Tenth Mountain Division wrote, "My platoon was attached to the Special Forces team that Dan was with. About seven months ago, I ran across the MWD website and saw a picture of Remmy and read that he had been retired and adopted. I cannot explain how that made me feel, knowing Remmy had survived since the last time I saw him and Dan in 2004–2005. We owe many thanks and probably our lives to Dan and Remmy. I am proud to have served with both of them. Thanks to Doug Davis for adopting one of our unsung heroes. The dogs do so much, and a nice fireplace to lie in front of is the least that we could do for them. Thanks again for bringing him into your home!"

Soon others who served with Remmy added the following comments: "Love Remmy! Saved my life, that's for sure!"

"Thank you, Dan and Remmy, for your service to our country. Without you there would be a lot less guys standing around talking about how bad we once were."

"Just incredible! That dog did more for the War on Terror tactically than most."

"The Warriors you just mentioned had their guardian angels fight with them day in and day out. And I believe Remmy has a human's soul; even IEDs on Roller Coaster Hill only gave them bruises."

"Give Remmy a treat from all the Cobras (soldiers with the Twenty-Fifty Infantry based in Hawaii) and ODA he saved."

"That brave K-9 saved our lives and helped us kill Taliban. So happy to see him living the good life!"

"I tell my daughters about the times Remmy saved mine and my squads' lives in DRW Afghanistan."

"These are two important people who helped make my safe return home from Afghanistan a reality."

One former serviceman wrote, "I just named my new puppy after Remmy, who led the way for my army platoon to conduct our missions."

REMMY'S RETIREMENT PARTY

As news of Dan finding Remmy spread, men who served with them in Afghanistan, began expressing a desire to also see the dog responsible for saving so many of their lives. One weekend just before Christmas, Doug and Pam traveled to Illinois with Remmy, where Dan and his wife hosted what was dubbed "Remmy's Retirement Party."

During dinner Davis learned that prior to meeting him, some of the men had decided that if they thought Remmy was not being well cared for, they were going to come to Michigan and dognap him. But once they saw the devotion exhibited between Doug and Remmy, their concerns were put to rest, especially when they learned that not only did he have a good home, but that he receives cold-laser treatments on a regular basis to help with his arthritis, and he even accompanied Doug when he went to his chiropractor appointments and, while there, was given his own special massage.

When the former unit commander first saw Remmy as he entered the room with his daughter, he instinctively reached back to shield her from the once-formidable warrior. He had difficulty believing that the now-docile dog standing in front of him was the same animal he knew in Afghanistan.

The weekend was filled with memories, laughter, and camaraderie as men who had served with Dan and Remmy traded war stories and lavished praise on the guest of honor. One of the men in particular told Doug, "You have no clue! That dog is one of the best bomb dogs I have ever worked with in my life. No dog ever compared to him. He really did save my life on several rough missions, finding IEDs, booby traps, as well as providing personal protection in crowds. After I rotated home, I do know that he was involved on several high-value targets to kill or capture senior Taliban commanders within Afghanistan, and he went on several other classified missions."

Another individual recounted the story of how sometime after Dan had returned to the United States, Remmy had been involved in a horrific dogfight with an Afghani fighting dog. He ultimately won the fight, but he had been left with injuries so severe that they caused him to be permanently removed from duty. This left everyone wondering how a dog who had proven himself to be such a valuable asset to the military was ever allowed to become embroiled in a fight in the first place.

Corporal Gio recalled the day when the Third Squad Second Platoon 2-5 infantry was on a mounted patrol with the SF group (Special Forces) they were attached to. He said, "We got some intel about some IEDs being placed on the route that we were taking, and so our convoy stopped to let some operators do a quick sweep of the area. When they finished their sweep, they were getting ready to mount back up when Remmy walked by our Humvee, and like always we talked to him, saying, 'Good boy, Remmy!' All of a sudden, he went in front of our vehicle and sat down. So we thought nothing of it and got ready to move out, when Dan yelled, 'STOP, STOP!' Remmy sat because that is what he is trained to do when he sniffs out an IED. We would have rolled right over the IED and died if it wasn't for Remmy. He saved our lives that day! SF found the IED where Remmy was sitting…literally two feet in front of our vehicle."

They all shared a good laugh when Dan told them about a painful lesson he learned while parachuting from a C130 airplane for the first time with Remmy. With Remmy in a harness attached to the front of Dan's body, they proceeded to jump from the plane, but Remmy became so excited he clamped his teeth into Dan's leg for the duration of that jump. From then on, whenever they parachuted, Dan made sure Remmy had a Kong in his mouth and was wearing a muzzle.

At the end of the party, everyone agreed to keep in touch with Doug and Remmy. On the trip back to Michigan, a tired and well-respected war hero, slept curled up in the back of the Davises' van, for most of the way back home.

Men who once served with Remmy attended his retirement party.

Remmy Takes on Hollywood

The story of Remmy's heroics and his reunion with Dan soon took on a life of its own, and one day Dan contacted Doug to inform him that a TV documentary featuring Remmy was in the works. In April of 2014, a film crew with Pilgrim Studios out of Hollywood California, along with movie and television personality R. Lee Ermey—known by many as "Gunny"—arrived at the Cherry Capital Airport in Traverse City to film a thirty-minute documentary based on Remmy's reunion with Dan. Dan flew in to take part in the filming, and Priscilla Miller, the writer whose article was responsible for Dan reuniting with Remmy, was invited and able to finally meet him. The documentary was later featured on the premier episode of *Saving Private K-9* and aired on the Sportsman Channel.

"Gunny" R. Lee Ermey, Doug, and Dan with the star of the show.

Doug, Pam, and Gunny watch as Dan and Remmy are reunited once again.

The writer whose article started it all looks on as the cameras roll.

THE CELEBRITY

With all of his new found fame, Remmy became quite a local celebrity and was invited to participate in a fundraiser for the World War II Honor Flights being held at Center Ice Arena in Traverse City. The original plan was to have him carry the puck in his mouth out onto the ice on Veterans' Night at the arena, but with Remmy not having any teeth, this wasn't possible. So it was decided that he would just accompany Dan, who was flying in from Illinois to be a guest speaker, out onto the ice.

Doug was worried about how Remmy would respond to walking on ice, especially in front of a crowd, so Pam took him to the arena every day for three straight weeks. They practiced walking around the ice rink together and attended some of the practice games until he became accustomed to the sounds of people playing hockey. He also made a lot of new friends during these visits, and once he discovered bits of popcorn that had been dropped on the floor of the arena stands by hockey fans, the arena became his favorite place to visit.

On the night of the event, Remmy and Dan were introduced to the crowd, but when the crowd erupted in applause and the hockey players lined up on either side of the arena, began slamming their hockey sticks against the ice, Remmy became so agitated he slipped out of his collar. Dan managed to grab a hold of him and put the collar back on, and then Doug immediately took Remmy off the ice and put him outside in the family van.

Ready for his debut at Center Ice Arena

THE PASSING OF A GREAT WARRIOR

O ne day while Pam was busy sewing in the basement, she heard a commotion upstairs and assumed Remmy was rambunctiously play-ing with his ball, but then suddenly, Remmy came stumbling down the stairs. She instantly knew he was in trouble. He was unable to walk on his own, so Pam managed to fashion a sling of sorts from some fabric she had been working on and somehow managed to carry him upstairs and get him into the family van. She called Doug, and he raced to meet her at the vet. Fortunately for Remmy, a new holistic veterinarian had joined their long-time vet's practice. After treating Remmy, he placed him on a holistic diet of sweet potatoes, broccoli, cottage cheese, blueberries, Greek yogurt, a mixture of Chinese herbs, and an egg every day. For a week Remmy had to be carried outside to relieve himself, but within a month his back had improved. He lost the extra weight he was carrying and was running around looking and acting like he was six years old again rather than a dog of fourteen. In what can best be described as a "labor of love," every week Pam cooked up about ten pounds of sweet potatoes for him, leaving Doug to joke that "the dog is eating better than we are!"

For several months Remmy continued to respond to his new diet, but ultimately the ravages of age took its toll. The day came when Doug had to send out the following dreaded e-mail to everyone who knew and loved Remmy. It read, "It was heartbreaking to let him go, but after a sudden illness, CWD Remmy left us yesterday afternoon. He had an amazing life, one with those he served with and one with us here in Traverse City, Michigan. He was always ready to meet new people, and he loved riding in the van. He loved it when he got to wear his service vest and work. Only a few days ago, he walked proudly into Munson Medical Center to meet some people in the surgical waiting room. He had the heart of a four-year-old pup and the body of a fourteen-year-old pup. He will be missed by all. He made a lot of very special friends here who always made him happy."

Upon learning of Remmy's passing, one of his former handlers said, "All working dogs are heroes, but Remmy was one in every sense of the word. While on the one rotation with my team, Remmy saved us from over twenty roadside bombs (IEDs) and booby-trapped rooms inside of homes the Taliban had set for us. We didn't suffer a single causality because of his actions. To put a price tag on lives saved is impossible. Because men were able to return home to be husbands to wives, fathers to their children, sons to their parents, and leaders within their communities. Some of them are still on active duty in Third Special Forces Group, Fort Bragg. Remmy went on to serve two more tours in Afghanistan, continuing to do his job until he couldn't from injuries. He was sent back to the United States and was eventually adopted by Doug and Pam Davis. Remmy received a very quiet and beautiful life because of their kindness and willingness to care for him through his last four plus years in northern Michigan. Danny and I were able to be reunited with Remmy in December 2013 after many years of searching for Remmy. At the official retirement party for Remmy, three of his handlers were able to be present to pay honor to a true special friend. It was amazing that he still remembered us and looked as happy as we were to see him also. Remmy passed on today, December 22, around 4:00 a.m. Rest well and God speed to one of the finest bomb dogs and protectors anyone could have asked to serve with."

Doug and Dan met again to say their final good-byes and to honor the hero dog of war they both loved so much. After they said their final good-byes to Remmy, Doug with Pam by his side, stood and watched as Remmy's former handler approached the flag-draped warrior, leaned over, and softly spoke to him for the last time.

Remmy lives on in the hearts of Doug, Pam, and all who knew and loved him.

Photo credit: Tom Vranich

All proceeds from the sale of this book go to support Mission K-9 Rescue and the Warrior's Path: PTSD Treatment and Therapy.

www.missionk9rescue.org

www.operationwarriorspath.org

Made in the USA
Middletown, DE
01 December 2016